TODAY'S SUPERSTARS

CC Sabathia

By Therese Shea

Gareth Stevens
Publishing

Please visit our Web site, www.garethstevens.com. For a free color catalog of all our high-quality books, call toll free 1-800-542-2595 or fax 1-877-542-2596.

Library of Congress Cataloging-in-Publication Data

Shea, Therese.
 CC Sabathia / Therese Shea.
    p. cm. — (Today's superstars)
 Includes bibliographical references and index.
 ISBN 978-1-4339-3987-7 (pbk.)
 ISBN 978-1-4339-3988-4 (6-pack)
 ISBN 978-1-4339-3986-0 (library binding)
 1. Sabathia, CC (Carsten Charles)—Juvenile literature 2. Baseball players—United States--Biography. 3. African American baseball players—United States—Biography. 4. Pitchers (Baseball)—United States—Biography. I. Title.
 GV865.S17S54 2011
 796.357092--dc22
 [B]

                         2010010176

First Edition

Published in 2011 by
Gareth Stevens Publishing
111 East 14th Street, Suite 349
New York, NY 10003

Copyright © 2011 Gareth Stevens Publishing

Designer: Daniel Hosek
Editor: Therese Shea

Photo credits: Cover, p. 1 Rich Pilling/Major League Baseball/Getty Images; pp. 4–5, 8, 34–35, 37 Nick Latham/Getty Images; pp. 6, 7, 33, 41 Jim Isaac/Getty Images; p. 9 Library of Congress; pp. 10, 15 Diamond Images/Getty Images; pp. 12, 18, 19, 26, 40 Brian Bahr/Getty Images; pp. 13, 14 (score card), 21, 31 Shutterstock.com; pp. 14 (baseball), 44 © Corbis; p. 16 Rick Stewart/Getty Images; pp. 20, 32 (bottom) Jed Jacobsohn/Getty Images; pp. 22–23, 27 Darren Hauck/Getty Images; p. 24 © Ezra Shaw/Getty Images; p. 25 Scott Schneider/Getty Images; pp. 28, 38 Al Messerschmidt/Getty Images; p. 30 Getty Images; p. 32 (top) Al Bello/Getty Images; p. 36 Jeff Zelevansky/Getty Images; p. 39 Chuck Solomon/ Getty Images; p. 46 G. Newman Lowrance/Getty Images.

Printed in the United States of America

CPSIA compliance information: Batch #CS10GS: For further information contact Gareth Stevens, New York, New York at 1-800-542-2595.

Contents

Words in the glossary appear in **bold** type the first time they are used in the text.

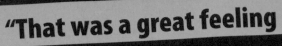

"That was a great feeling

TO HAVE THE STADIUM ROCKING."

—CC Sabathia, on pitching Game 1 of the 2009 ALCS

CC Sabathia celebrates after striking out a Los Angeles Angel during Game 1 of the 2009 ALCS.

Chapter 1
Pitching History

October 16, 2009. It was a cold, windy night in Yankee Stadium. CC Sabathia, the New York Yankees pitcher, tried not to let the weather bother him. After all, playing in October meant the Yankees were still alive in the **postseason**. They had beaten the Minnesota Twins in the American League Division Series (ALDS). Now they were taking on the Los Angeles Angels of Anaheim in the American League Championship Series (ALCS).

The Yankees had a chance at going to — and maybe winning — the World Series. But first they had to get past the Angels, the American League West division champions for the third year in a row. Sabathia took the mound in Game 1 of the best-of-seven series.

Power Pitcher

After eight innings, Sabathia had allowed just four hits. Of these, one run was scored. Over 49,000 fans chanted his name: "CC, CC!" The Yankees won the first game, 4–1.

Manager Joe Girardi gave Sabathia only 3 days to rest. In Game 4, with the Yankees leading the series two games to one, Sabathia threw 101 pitches. He gave up just five hits. The Yankees won, 10–1. Angels fielder Torii Hunter said, "We thought 3 days' rest would be tough on him. But he actually got better."

Fact File

CC didn't pick his jersey number (52). It's just the number he got from the Cleveland Indians, his first MLB team.

About CC

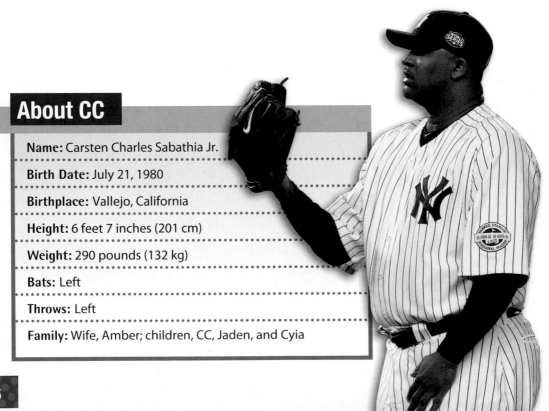

Name: Carsten Charles Sabathia Jr.

Birth Date: July 21, 1980

Birthplace: Vallejo, California

Height: 6 feet 7 inches (201 cm)

Weight: 290 pounds (132 kg)

Bats: Left

Throws: Left

Family: Wife, Amber; children, CC, Jaden, and Cyia

Yankees Win!

After five games in the ALCS, the Yankees were ahead three games to two. Could the Angels tie it up in Game 6?

On October 25, 2009, the Yankees defeated the Angels 5–2. The winning team jumped off the bench and streamed out onto the field. They hugged and piled on top of each other.

CC Sabathia was in the middle of it all. His team was going to the 2009 World Series, and he was a big reason why. Sabathia was named the ALCS Most Valuable Player (MVP).

TRUE OR FALSE?

CC Sabathia was the first Yankee to win both the Cy Young Award and ALCS MVP.

For answers, see page 46.

▼ The New York Yankees celebrate after winning the 2009 ALCS.

The Pitching Team

A Major League Baseball (MLB) team has many pitchers. A pitcher's arm gets tired after pitching several innings. Managers plan a rotation, or a list of their best pitchers in order. The pitchers in the rotation start **consecutive** games in turn. The pitcher from the first game usually has 4 or 5 days of rest before his next game. Some pitchers, such as Sabathia, are starting pitchers. They start the game and play several innings. Other pitchers—called relief pitchers—take over in the middle or towards the end of the game.

A. J. Burnett, pitcher

Joba Chamberlain, pitcher

CC Sabathia, pitcher

Derek Jeter, shortstop

Xavier Nady, outfielder

Andy Pettitte, pitcher

TRUE OR FALSE?

CC Sabathia weighed less than any other pitcher in the MLB in 2009.

CC's Cities

The 2009 season was Sabathia's first with the New York Yankees. The year before, he played the first half of the season with the Cleveland Indians, where he had started his career. Then, he joined the Milwaukee Brewers for the second half of the season. In all three cities, he helped his teams make it to the postseason. Winning the ALCS with the Yankees was the furthest he had ever gotten in postseason play. Could the Yankees win the World Series with their new starting pitcher?

What It Takes

It takes more than talent to make it to the World Series. It requires months of practicing pitches and years of perfecting them. Add to that years spent on school and **minor league** teams.

CC Sabathia is among the most gifted players in the MLB. The story of his career isn't the story of an instant superstar. It's the story of a talented young man whose positive attitude and hard work helped him become one of the most popular baseball players today.

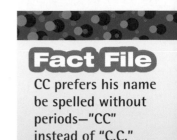

What Is an ERA?

An earned run average (ERA) is a baseball statistic, or number value. An earned run is any run scored as a result of pitching. A run isn't "earned" if it's scored due to a fielder's **error** or a catcher's mistake. An ERA is the number of earned runs divided by the number of innings pitched, then multiplied by 9. A pitcher with a 3.00 ERA allows an average of 3 runs per game. The lower the ERA, the better the pitcher. The lowest career ERA was 1.82 by Chicago White Sox pitcher Ed Walsh (played 1904–1917).

Ed Walsh

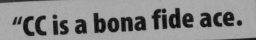

"CC is a bona fide ace.

THAT'S WHY HE'S THE MVP."

—outfielder Johnny Damon

Sabathia never throws the same pitch twice to a good batter.

Chapter 2
Born Athlete

Born on July 21, 1980, CC Sabathia grew up in Vallejo, California. Life wasn't perfect. There were drugs and violence on the streets. Sabathia didn't get mixed up in these things. He was too busy playing football, basketball, and baseball.

Abe Hobbs, Sabathia's coach at Vallejo High School, said, "(CC) came from a pretty rough area in Vallejo, and a lot of guys didn't end up successful from that area. He's always been levelheaded."

Sabathia owes much of his success to people like Hobbs and to his parents. Without them, CC wouldn't be thrilling baseball fans with his pitching today. CC would be the first to admit it.

Margie

Sabathia had a lot of support from his biggest fan—his mother, Margie. She taught him to believe in himself. Margie played catch in the backyard with Sabathia until his fastball almost broke her hand! Sabathia said, "She understands the game big-time. I've been able to talk about sports with her—all sports—since I was 12."

Margie taught Sabathia an important lesson for an athlete. "Be **confident**, but be humble, too." She meant that he should believe in himself, but respect others as well.

▼ Margie Sabathia taught CC to be thankful for his talent.

12

Learning to Keep His Cool

Coach Hobbs told a story about CC and Margie's relationship. It shows what a good coach she was. Sabathia had hit a ball out of play during a game. He angrily threw his helmet to the ground. Margie ran over and spoke to him. Sabathia then ran to his coach. He promised it would never happen again. "And it didn't," said Hobbs. A good player takes the bad with the good. This was a good lesson in **sportsmanship**.

Everyone's Watching CC

Many more people than Margie watched Sabathia grow up. Cleveland Indians **scout** Paul Cogan remembers going to several of Sabathia's high school baseball games. Cogan also went to Sabathia's football and basketball games to see his all-around talent. Cogan wondered if Sabathia should be a first baseman rather than a pitcher. Pitchers don't usually bat in the American League (AL), and Sabathia could really hit. Cogan remembers a game in which Sabathia hit the ball so far that no one ever found it!

Fact File

Margie Sabathia calls her son "Dude."

Baseball Letters

When you read about a baseball game, some terms are shortened. Here are a few short terms and what they mean:

shortened term	full term	meaning
BB	base on balls, or walk	an award of first base given to a batter who, during his time at bat, receives four pitches outside the strike zone
RBI	run batted in	credit given to a batter when his batting results in a run being scored
SHO	shutout	a complete game pitched without allowing a run
H	hit	any hit by a batter that results in the batter reaching first base
K or SO	strikeout	credit given to a pitcher for throwing three strikes against a batter
W	win	credit given to a starting pitcher who has pitched at least five innings, whose team is in the lead when he is replaced, and whose team wins

TRUE OR FALSE?

About 2,500 people watched the opening game of Sabathia's last high school season.

Who Wants CC?

By his junior year of high school, Sabathia was 6 feet 6 inches (198 cm) tall and weighed 245 pounds (111 kg). Some scouts weren't sure that a pitcher of Sabathia's size would do well in the MLB. But he could really move! For his last high school season, his pitching record was 6 wins and 0 losses with 82 strikeouts and an amazingly low 0.77 ERA.

Which Way to Go?

Sabathia received an offer from the University of Hawaii. He had the chance to play both football and baseball for the school. He knew the Cleveland Indians were interested, too. By the end of high school, Sabathia faced choices: football or baseball? College or pros?

Sabathia was selected twentieth overall in the 1998 **amateur** baseball **draft**. He had made a choice, and the choice was MLB baseball.

Because Sabathia is so tall, he throws the ball "downhill" to the plate.

15

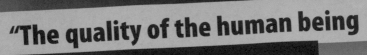

"The quality of the human being **MATCHES THE TALENT.**"

—Cleveland Indians general manager Mark Shapiro

CC Sabathia is known for wearing his cap a certain way—with the brim wide and flat.

Chapter 3

On the Mound in Cleveland

Most players chosen in the MLB draft perfect their skills on minor league "farm teams." These serve as training teams to get players ready to compete in the major league. Players who were stars on their high school or college teams learn to play against equally talented people. Sabathia played on five different farm teams before taking the mound in Cleveland.

In 2000, Sabathia led all Indians minor league pitchers in strikeouts with 159 in 146 innings. By 2001, it was time to see if his big-league talent was a match to his MLB team. Just 20 years old, Sabathia was the youngest pitcher in the MLB that year.

The Rookie

In 2001, Sabathia had a good **rookie** year. He had a 17–5 win-loss record with a 4.39 ERA in 33 starts. He was among the top 10 pitchers in wins and strikeouts. However, he was also second in the American League for the number of times he allowed batters to walk.

That year, the Indians made it as far as the ALDS. They lost the series to the Seattle Mariners. However, Sabathia won the only game he pitched. He had proven himself. Sabathia signed a 4-year contract with Cleveland.

Dealing with Fame and Fortune

In 2001, Sabathia was no longer a kid in Vallejo. He was a rich athlete. He began going to parties. He wore expensive jewelry. One night changed all that.

Sabathia was robbed at gunpoint in May 2001. He changed his life immediately. He asked his girlfriend, Amber, to marry him that same night. Sabathia said the robbery "was really a blessing in disguise. To have a gun to your head is scary, but it put everything in order." From then on, family was first in his life.

Rookie No More

Sabathia didn't start as an ace pitcher his second year. The first part of the season left him with an ERA of 5.45. However, he turned it around. In his last 11 games, he threw for a 2.54 ERA. Again, he was second in the AL in walks. It was something he had to work on.

In the 2003 season, Sabathia pitched at least five innings in 29 of 30 starts. He threw his first major league shutout on August 15, 2003. Pitching all nine innings, he didn't allow the Tampa Bay Rays a single run. Overall, his ERA was 3.60. Sabathia was named an AL All-Star for the first time.

Sabathia works with the catcher to decide which pitches to throw.

Two Solid Seasons

▲ Sabathia and catcher Ivan Rodriguez talk on the mound during the 2004 All-Star Game.

TRUE OR FALSE?

CC Sabathia danced with the Oakland Ballet in *The Nutcracker.*

Playing against the Detroit Tigers in July 2004, Sabathia won his fiftieth career game. He also collected his second shutout. For the second year in a row, he was chosen to play in the All-Star Game.

The 2005 season was Sabathia's fifth straight year of double-digit wins. During the last 8 weeks of the season, he had 9 wins and 1 loss with a 2.24 ERA. The Indians gave him a contract for another 2 years.

A 2006 Breakthrough

Sabathia pitched for a 1.20 ERA in his first six games of 2006. He was named the AL Pitcher of the Month in May. His 3.22 ERA for the season was the third lowest in the AL.

Sabathia worked on keeping his pitches over home plate. He cut his number of walks by 18 from 2005 and by 51 from his rookie year. His other statistics, such as strikeouts (172) and shutouts (2), were among the best in the AL. He led MLB pitchers with six complete games.

Remembering Vallejo

While Sabathia's star was rising in the MLB, he remembered his hometown, Vallejo, California. He bought a batting cage for his high school. He paid for little league field improvements. Sometimes he even worked out with the high school baseball team.

Sabathia wants to start a "baseball academy" in northern California. Students would learn to play baseball while setting aside time for schoolwork.

"I was excited . . .

I WAS SURPRISED."

—CC Sabathia, on winning his Cy Young Award

Sabathia raises his arms to Milwaukee fans after pitching a complete game on September 28, 2008.

Chapter 4

A Cy Young Pitcher

A starting pitcher may throw 120 pitches a game. Working with the catcher, the pitcher decides what pitch to throw. Should it be a fastball, curveball, sinker, or another pitch? The ball is often thrown faster than 90 miles (145 km) per hour. It should cross over home plate, which is 60 feet 6 inches (18.4 m) away. If the ball is too far from the plate and the batter doesn't swing, the **umpire** calls a ball. If he calls four balls, the batter walks to first base. Meanwhile, the pitcher must have his eye on runners to make sure they don't steal bases.

Clearly, a good pitcher does more than just pitch. His position calls for a lot of responsibility. The Cy Young Award is an annual pitching honor. It's given only to the very best pitchers in the MLB.

A Standout Year

The 2007 season was the best yet for Sabathia. He threw an MLB-high 241 innings. His win-loss record was 19–7 with a 3.21 ERA and 209 strikeouts.

The Indians made it as far as the ALCS. There, Sabathia found he still had more to learn. He lost two of three games he pitched against the Boston Red Sox with a 10.45 ERA and 7 walks. "I can definitely say I was trying to do too much," Sabathia said. "Just trying to make perfect pitches."

TRUE OR FALSE?

Sabathia was the only Indians pitcher to win the Cy Young Award.

DENTON T. (CY) YOUNG
CLEVELAND (N) 1890-98
ST. LOUIS (N) 1899-1900
BOSTON (A) 1901-08
CLEVELAND (A) 1909-11
BOSTON (N) 1911
ONLY PITCHER IN FIRST HUNDRED
YEARS OF BASEBALL TO WIN 500 GAMES.
AMONG HIS 511 VICTORIES WERE 3
NO-HIT SHUTOUTS. PITCHED PERFECT
GAME MAY 5, 1904, NO OPPOSING
BATSMAN REACHING FIRST BASE.

The Cy Young Award

Denton True "Cy" Young pitched for five different major league teams from 1890 to 1911. Young currently holds the MLB records for most career innings pitched (7,355), most career games started (815), most complete games (749), and most wins (511).

The Cy Young Award winners are chosen by the Baseball Writers Association of America. From 1956 to 1966, only one winner was chosen. Rules were changed in 1967 to honor the best pitcher from each league.

A Team Player

Sabathia was a leader in the 2007 season. "Maybe the most influential leadership he demonstrated this year was how he handled the stretch of five to seven games where he got almost no run support," said Cleveland's general manager Mark Shapiro. "He never pointed fingers, never felt sorry for himself . . . and continued to contribute and pull for our team's victories, not worrying about his own individual performance." For his leadership and pitching skills, Sabathia won the 2007 Cy Young Award.

Fact File

The Sporting News chose Sabathia as its Pitcher of the Year in 2007. This award is older than the Cy Young Award.

▼ **The Cy Young Award is the highest honor for an MLB pitcher.**

CC Thanks Cleveland

When CC Sabathia left Cleveland, he bought an ad in the sports section of Cleveland's newspaper, *The Plain Dealer*. It said: "Thank you for 10 great years . . . You've touched our lives with your kindness, love, and generosity. We are forever grateful! It's been a privilege and an honor!"

"Wow, that just blows me away," Indians pitcher Paul Byrd said. "What a cool thing to do by a really great guy."

Moving to Milwaukee

Sabathia began the 2008 season with Cleveland. By July, his win-loss record was just 6–8, with a 3.83 ERA. The Indians had fallen in the standings. Believing they needed batting power, they traded Sabathia to the Milwaukee Brewers for four players. The Brewers needed Sabathia's pitching arm to climb to the top of the National League Central Division.

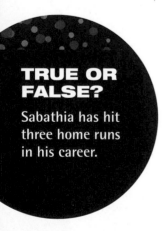

TRUE OR FALSE?

Sabathia has hit three home runs in his career.

The "CC Surge"

In 2008, the Brewers wanted to reach the postseason for the first time in 26 years. "We're expecting . . . a 'CC **surge**,' " said Brewers vice president Rick Schlesinger. Brewers fans were excited to see their new pitcher perform. Sabathia delivered. After 17 amazing games in Milwaukee, his record was 11–2 with a 1.65 ERA. He pitched seven complete games and three shutouts. Sabathia led the MLB in innings pitched, complete games, and shutouts.

The Brewers made it to the National League Division Series. However, they lost to the Philadelphia Phillies, who went on to win the World Series.

Fact File

In 2008, Sabathia had 11 hits and 6 RBIs as a Milwaukee Brewer.

▼ Sabathia celebrates after the Brewers clinch a spot in the 2008 postseason.

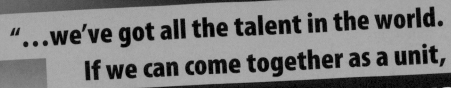

"…we've got all the talent in the world. If we can come together as a unit, **I THINK WE'LL BE UNSTOPPABLE.**"

—CC Sabathia

Sabathia is a big reason why the New York Yankees reached the 2009 World Series.

Chapter 5

CC, New York Yankee

After the 2008 season, Sabathia had decisions to make. His contract was over with Milwaukee. Many thought he would go back to California.

Sabathia got a call from the East Coast. The New York Yankees' general manager offered him a deal. Then, the Los Angeles Angels promised to match it. The Yankees raised the offer by $21 million. Sabathia's contract was the largest ever offered to a pitcher. The Angels couldn't match the amount. The "gentle giant" of the MLB and his wife, Amber, discussed raising their family in New York. After talking to other players, Sabathia accepted the Yankees' offer. He was now a New York Yankee.

The Offer

The Yankees had missed the 2008 playoffs. They had watched with interest as Sabathia led Milwaukee into the postseason. They wanted the big pitcher who had become a batter's nightmare. Sabathia agreed to a 7-year deal for $161 million.

Sabathia bonded with his new team. He remarked, "I like to hang out with my teammates . . . get to know them." During the Yankees' 2009 spring training, he went to Disney World with pitcher Joba Chamberlain. He organized fishing trips and Orlando Magic games with other teammates, too.

Fact File

CC's nickname is "Dub."

▼ Sabathia and Joba Chamberlain (right) bond during 2009 spring training.

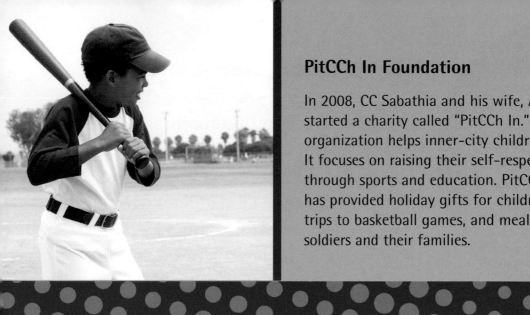

PitCCh In Foundation

In 2008, CC Sabathia and his wife, Amber, started a charity called "PitCCh In." The organization helps inner-city children. It focuses on raising their self-respect through sports and education. PitCCh In has provided holiday gifts for children, trips to basketball games, and meals for soldiers and their families.

A Low-Key Yankee

The New York Yankees, including such legends as Babe Ruth and Lou Gehrig, made "America's pastime" a worldwide sport. "I think everybody knows what the Yankee history is," Sabathia said.

Fact File

Sabathia chose to live outside of New York City. He bought a home in a small town in New Jersey.

Some players love the attention and fame that come with the pinstriped New York Yankees uniform. Sabathia isn't one of these. Teammates and reporters are often surprised by his relaxed manner. Sabathia shrugs. "That's kind of how I am," he says. "I don't figure to get into too much trouble . . . I just do my thing and try to help the team win."

New Stadium, New Start

The 2009 season was historic. The new Yankee Stadium had been completed. The old stadium had been the site of 26 Yankees World Series Championships. Mickey Mantle, Joe DiMaggio, Roger Maris, and other "Bronx Bombers" had set records there. The new stadium meant a new beginning.

Sabathia received word that he would pitch the home opener in the new stadium as well as the season opener in Baltimore. He would begin a new chapter in Yankees history for all Yankees fans.

▼ The new Yankee Stadium was built next to the original stadium.

original Yankee Stadium

new Yankee Stadium

The Pressure Is On

With money comes pressure. Sabathia was making a lot of money with the Yankees. Yankees fans were ready to support him. In the beginning of the season, sales of his jersey ranked third at the team store. Did he deserve the contract and support? Only time would tell.

The pressure didn't seem to affect Sabathia. He behaved much the same as the young Vallejo High School star he had been. However, his pitching arm was much more dangerous. "He's a workhorse," said outfielder Johnny Damon. "Adding CC makes us a serious contender again."

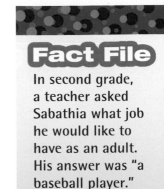

CC's Favorites

Musicians: Jay-Z and E40

Way to Relax: video games

Athlete Growing Up: Ken Griffey Jr.

Football Team: Oakland Raiders

City Away from Home: Chicago, Illinois

Ballpark Away from Home: Safeco Field (Seattle, Washington)

Holidays: Christmas and Thanksgiving

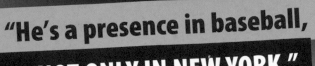

"He's a presence in baseball, **NOT ONLY IN NEW YORK.**"

—Yankees pitcher Joba Chamberlain

Sabathia tips his hat to the crowd during the 2009 American League Division Series.

Chapter 6

Slow Start, Fantastic Finish

Even superstars have bad days. Unfortunately, Sabathia had a bad day on April 6, 2009—the season opener. The Yankees played the Orioles in Baltimore. In a little over four innings, Sabathia gave up eight hits, six runs, and five walks. He sat out the rest of the game and watched the Yankees lose, 10–5. He also lost the home opener to Cleveland, 10–2.

People who thought these games showed Sabathia's worth were wrong. His best performance came about a month later. On May 8, 2009, Sabathia gave up just four hits in a complete shutout of the Orioles. The Yankees' batters contributed to the 4–0 win.

A Winning Season

After the victory in Baltimore, Sabathia continued to do his part for the Yankees. In August and September, he posted a 9–0 record with a 2.04 ERA. By the season's end, he had pitched 230 innings and led the AL with 19 wins.

Manager Joe Girardi said, "He doesn't seem to get tired around 90 to 100 pitches . . . that's what's so impressive about him." The Yankees ended the season with a 103–59 record at the top of the American League East.

▼ Sabathia works hard to throw each pitch with power and perfect aim.

CC's Success

The playoffs were Sabathia's next challenge. His past postseason pitching was discouraging. In the four postseason games he pitched for Cleveland and Milwaukee in 2007 and 2008, he gave up 20 runs in 19 innings.

▲ Sabathia and Mark Teixeira celebrate winning the 2009 ALCS.

But he was a better pitcher now. He won his only start against the Minnesota Twins in the ALDS. He earned an MVP award in the ALCS. In 16 innings against the Angels, he gave up just two runs and threw 12 strikeouts. The Yankees won the ALCS in six games.

Fact File
Sabathia says he would be a police officer if he didn't play baseball.

By the Numbers

1.98 ERA in the 2009 postseason

7 years in his contract with the Yankees

20th pick overall in the 1998 amateur draft

52 on his jersey

85 percent of writers voted for him for the 2007 Cy Young Award

$161.1 million contract with the Yankees

On to the World Series

On October 29, 2009, the Yankees met the Philadelphia Phillies in the opening game of the World Series. Sabathia was pitching. Although he only allowed four hits in seven innings, New York lost to Philadelphia, 6–1.

Sabathia took responsibility for the loss. "I was able to battle back and make some pitches when I needed to, but that's not at all how I've been pitching." The Yankees won the next two games with A. J. Burnett and Andy Pettitte on the mound.

How Big Should a Pitcher Be?

Sabathia practices and exercises nearly every day. However, many people still question his weight. They wonder if he would be an even better pitcher if he were slimmer. Others point out that he learned to pitch as a large person. If he lost weight, he might not be as powerful. This has happened to other pitchers.

Some think Sabathia's large body helps hide the path of the ball. His height and long arms allow him to reach toward home plate. If Sabathia's performance starts to go downhill, he may change his weight. But for now, he's just right.

The Yankees Win!

In Game 4, Sabathia allowed 3 runs, but left the mound with the Yankees in the lead. Sluggers Alex Rodriquez and Johnny Damon sealed the win in the ninth inning. The Yankees took a 3–1 series lead.

The Yankees lost Game 5. Game 6 was a team effort. Hideki Matsui's home run gave him his sixth RBI of the World Series. Andy Pettitte and Mariano Rivera pitched the team to a 7–3 win and the Yankees' first World Series Championship since 2000.

Humble as always, Sabathia said, "We've got a bunch of talent in here and a bunch of guys who get along and play well together. This is what happened."

▲ Sabathia and Mark Teixeira (right) greet fans at the Yankees' victory parade after the 2009 World Series.

TRUE OR FALSE?

Sabathia and Philadelphia Phillies pitcher Cliff Lee played together in Milwaukee.

Timeline

1980   Carsten Charles Sabathia Jr. is born on July 21 in Vallejo, California.

1998   Sabathia is picked by the Cleveland Indians in the amateur draft.

2001   Sabathia makes his first major league start.

2003   Sabathia is chosen for the All-Star Game for the first time.

2007 Sabathia wins the American League Cy Young Award.

2008 Sabathia is traded to the Milwaukee Brewers.

2008 Sabathia signs with the New York Yankees.

2009 Sabathia wins the MVP award for the American League Championship Series.

2009 Sabathia helps the Yankees win the World Series.

Glossary

amateur: someone who does something without pay

confident: believing one can succeed

consecutive: following one after another with no break

draft: the choosing of players for a team or teams

error: a mistake in baseball when a play that should have led to an out or stopped a runner from reaching a base doesn't

minor league: a league of professional teams that do not belong to the major league

postseason: games played after the regular season

rookie: a player who is in the first year of playing a sport

scout: someone who searches for people with great skills in a sport

sportsmanship: a way of behaving in sports that includes respecting rules, others, and the outcome of a game

surge: a sudden increase in something

umpire: an official who watches a game and makes sure rules are followed

To Find Out More

Books

Doeden, Matt. *The Best of Pro Baseball*. Mankato, MN: Capstone Press, 2010.

New York Post. *The Best! Yankees Bring the World Series Title Back Home*. Chicago, IL: Triumph Books, 2009.

Stone, Lynn M. *Pitchers*. Vero Beach, FL: Rourke Publishing, 2008.

Web Sites

CC Sabathia's Official Site
ccsabathia52.com
Sabathia's site provides news, biography, photos, and contact information.

Major League Baseball Statistics and History
www.baseball-reference.com
Read information about MLB players and teams as well as minor league statistics.

The Official Site of Major League Baseball
mlb.mlb.com
Find out information, get statistics, see videos, and learn history for all MLB teams.

Championships and Awards*

All-Star
2003, 2004, 2007

American League Cy Young Award
2007

Players Choice Awards Outstanding Pitcher of the Year
2007

The Sporting News AL Pitcher of the Year
2007

MLB Clutch Performer of the Year
2008

ALCS MVP
2009

World Series Champion
2009

* As of March 2010

Source Notes

p. 4 Mel Antonen, "Sabathia Overwhelms Angels in Game 1 of ALCS with 4–1 Win," *USA TODAY*, October 17, 2009, http://www.usatoday.com/sports/baseball/playoffs/2009-10-16-alcs-game-1_N.htm.

p. 6 Paul White, "Yanks Blast Angels Behind CC, A-Rod for 3–1 Lead," *USA TODAY*, October 21, 2009, http://www.usatoday.com/sports/baseball/playoffs/2009-10-20-alcs-game-4_N.htm.

p. 10 Associated Press, "Sabathia Earns ALCS MVP Nod," ESPN, October 25, 2009, http://sports.espn.go.com/mlb/playoffs/2009/news/story?id=4594974.

p. 11 Anthony McCarron, "The Real CC Sabathia: New Yankee an Ace Off Field," *New York Daily News*, December 11, 2008, http://www.nydailynews.com/sports/baseball/yankees/2008/12/10/2008-12-10_the_real_cc_sabathia_new_yankee_an_ace_o.html.

p. 12 The Official Site of Pitcher CC Sabathia, "About CC," http://ccsabathia52.com/about.html (accessed January 9, 2010).

p. 13 McCarron.

p. 16 McCarron.

p. 18 S. L. Price, "Big Love 'CC'," *Sports Illustrated*, April 6, 2009, http://sportsillustrated.cnn.com/vault/article/magazine/MAG1153909/index.htm.

p. 22 Associated Press, "Sabathia Only Second Indians Pitcher to Win Cy Young," ESPN, November 14, 2007, http://sports.espn.go.com/mlb/news/story?id=3108321.

p. 24 "Sabathia Only Second."

p. 25 "Sabathia Only Second."

p. 26 Associated Press, "CC Sabathia Says 'Thank You' to Cleveland Fans," *USA TODAY*, July 7, 2008, http://www.usatoday.com/sports/baseball/2008-07-30-1768344374_x.htm.

p. 27 Jack Curry, "Looking to Postseason, Brewers Trade for Sabathia," *New York Times*, July 8, 2008, http://www.nytimes.com/2008/07/08/sports/baseball/08brewers.html.

p. 28 Tyler Kepner, "Yankees' Ace Has Become a Leader," *New York Times*, March 22, 2009, http://query.nytimes.com/gst/fullpage.html?res=9C02E5D9173AF930A15750C0A96F9C8B63.

p. 30 Kepner.

p. 31 (first quote) Kepner. (second quote) Bryan Hoch, "CC Gets Both Opening Day Assignments," MLB.com, March 26, 2009, http://mlb.mlb.com/news/article.jsp?ymd=20090326&content_id=4067964&vkey=news_mlb&fext=.jsp&c_id=mlb.

p. 33 Tyler Kepner, "7 Years and $161 Million, and They're Not Done Yet," *New York Times*, December 11, 2008, http://query.nytimes.com/gst/fullpage.html?res=9D06E0DF1E3EF932A25751C1A96E9C8B63.

p. 34 Hoch.

p. 36 Jared Diamond, "CC Rolls to Lead Yanks to Seventh Straight," Yankees.com, May 5, 2009, http://newyork.yankees.mlb.com/news/article.jsp?ymd=20090519&content_id=4817428&vkey=recap&fext=.jsp&c_id=nyy.

p. 38 Tyler Kepner, "Lee Outpitches Sabathia in Game 1," *New York Times*, October 29, 2009, http://www.nytimes.com/2009/10/29/sports/baseball/29series.html.

p. 39 Jenifer Langosch, "Start Spreadin' the Clues: Why Yanks Won," MLB.com, November 5, 2009, http://mlb.mlb.com/news/article.jsp?ymd=20091104&content_id=7621016&vkey=ps2009news&fext=.jsp&c_id=mlb.

True or False Answers

Page 7 True.

Page 8 False. Sabathia was the heaviest pitcher in the MLB at 290 pounds (132 kg).

Page 12 True.

Page 14 True.

Page 19 False. Sabathia was chosen for the team but only played one pre-Olympic game.

Page 20 True.

Page 24 False. Cleveland pitcher Gaylord Perry won the award in 1972.

Page 26 True. As of 2009.

Page 32 True.

Page 39 True.

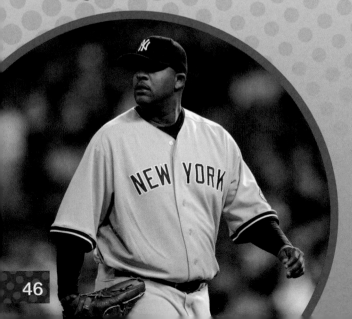

Index

About the Author

Therese Shea has written over one hundred children's books, including sports biographies of hockey, soccer, and basketball superstars. She attended Providence College in Rhode Island, where she was witness to the great Yankees–Red Sox rivalry in action. Therese now lives in Buffalo, New York, with her husband, Mark.